Introducing

GEORGIAN GLASGOW

How Glasgow flourished

Glasgow Museums

First published in 2014 by Glasgow Museums to accompany the exhibition *How Glasgow Flourished, 1714–1837* at Kelvingrove Art Gallery and Museum.

ISBN 978-1-908638-06-9

British Library Cataloguing in Publication Data

A catalogue record for this book is available from the British Library

Written by Fiona Hayes, Anthony Lewis, and Isobel McDonald

Designed by Fiona MacDonald

Edited by Fiona MacLeod

Photography by Jim Dunn and Maureen Kinnear

Printed in Scotland by Allander

Acknowledgments

P.37 © Science Museum / Science & Society Picture Library

P.38 © Renfrewshire Arts and Museums

P.66 © The University of Glasgow Library, Special Collections

With thanks to Development & Regeneration Services, Glasgow City Council.

Front cover images:
Detail from *The Woman Shop Keeper*
about 1790–1800
Temp.7685

The Trongate of Glasgow in 1774
James Brown, after Maclure & Macdonald
1906.12

Plan of Glasgow, 1775
PP.1982.202.1

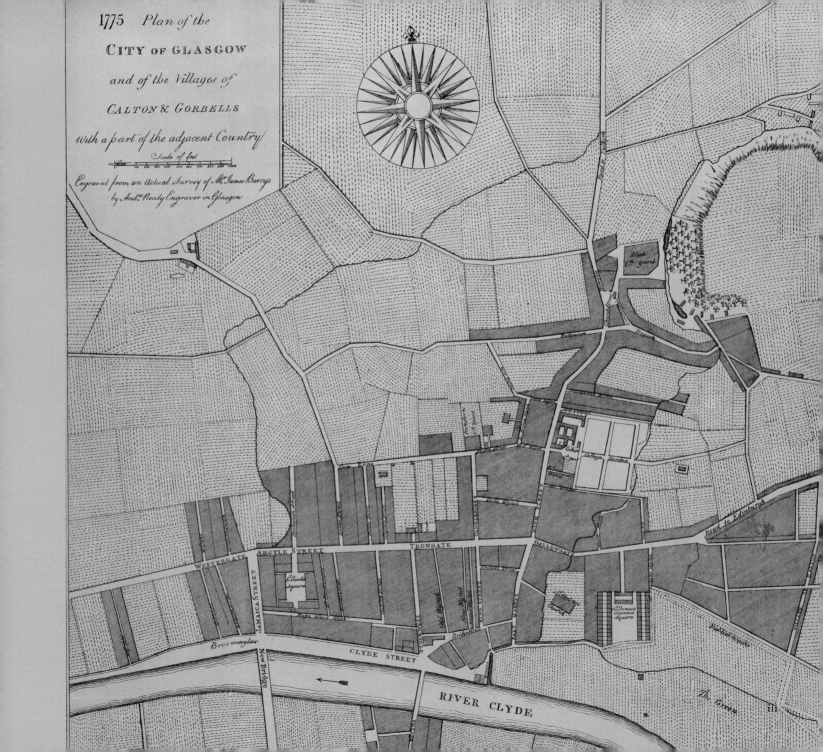

1775   Plan of the

CITY OF GLASGOW

and of the Villages of

CALTON & GORBELLS

With a part of the adjacent Country

Scale of feet

Engraved from an Actual Survey of Mr James Barry's
by Andw Ready Engraver in Glasgow

High Chh yard

Rottenrow   Drygate

College   College Garden

Duke Street

Bells Wynd

Andersons Street

High Street

Road to Edinburgh

WESTERGATE   ARGYLE STREET   TRONGATE   GALLOWGAT

S Enochs
Square

Rope Work Lane

JAMAICA STREET

Stockwell Street

Old Wynd

New Wynd

King Street

Saltmarket Street

Prince's Street

St James's
intended
Square

College
Church

Butlick Walk

Broomylaw

New Bridge

CLYDE STREET

Bridgegate

The Green

←

RIVER CLYDE

iii

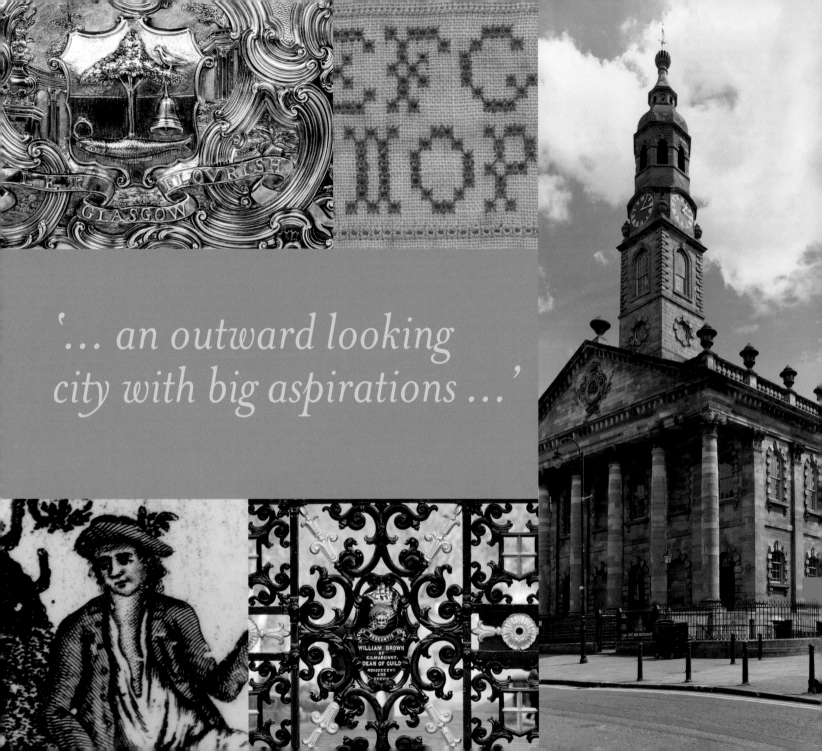

'... an outward looking
city with big aspirations ...'

FOREWORD

These sculptures of a lion and a unicorn were brought from Glasgow University's original location in the east end (pictured opposite) to its present site in the 1800s.

This book celebrates Georgian Glasgow, which dates from 1714 to 1837 and encompasses the reigns of the Hanoverian kings – George I, George II, George III, George IV and William IV. It is an important but often overlooked period of the city's history.

Daniel Defoe famously wrote of the city, 'tis the cleanest and beautifullest, and best built city in Britain, London excepted.' This is a striking contrast with the more familiar image of Glasgow, dominated by heavy industry, that came later.

The city Defoe describes dates from the start of the Georgian era, a period during which it underwent a dramatic expansion in size and status, laying the foundation of the place we see today.

But even then it was an outward looking city, with big aspirations and growing overseas interests. Glasgow's merchants prospered during this time, dominating international trade in tobacco, sugar and textiles. It was also the era of the Industrial Revolution, when mechanization shifted production away from small-scale cottage industries to mass production in factories. Along with this came social change, the birth of consumer culture and a flourishing of the arts.

To highlight its importance in shaping the city's history and landscape, the Georgian period was selected as the focus of a major exhibition at Kelvingrove Art Gallery and Museum, *How Glasgow Flourished, 1714–1837*, during the XX Commonwealth Games in Glasgow in 2014.

Introducing Georgian Glasgow features a selection of the objects dating from the Georgian period which are in the city's museum and archive collections – including paintings, prints, furniture, costume and textiles, jewellery, silverware, musical instruments and other domestic items. We hope this book offers a glimpse into Glasgow's past through a range of objects that help tell the story of how it grew and flourished in the 1700s and early 1800s.

If you would like to learn more about Glasgow and investigate your own or your family's connections with the city, we encourage you to use Glasgow Life's archive and rare book collections, visit the Family History Centre in the Mitchell Library and explore the museum collection in more detail.

Duncan Dornan
Senior Museums Manager
(Public Programming and Customer Service)

The Colledge of Glasgow,
date unknown,
(after Slezer)
1929.11.b

The COLLEDGE of GLASGOW.

Dr Anthony Lewis

INTRODUCTION

In the early 1700s Glasgow experienced an economic boom, which profoundly shaped the city during the Georgian period.

This was the age of the merchants. Although best known as the 'Tobacco Lords', in practice Glasgow's merchants had much wider business interests, including sugar, textiles, banking and even herring. Glaswegian merchants traded across Britain's growing Empire. They dominated the tobacco industry and by the late 1700s were handling well over half of Britain's entire trade in tobacco from the Americas.

Great fortunes were made, but they were also lost as a result of financial crashes and the lengthy wars that punctuated the 1700s and early 1800s, including the Wars of American Independence and the Napoleonic wars. Merchants profited from direct or indirect participation in the slave trade, meaning that Glasgow's wealth in the 1700s came in part from the labours of people who had been enslaved.

Geography also played a role in Glasgow's economic success. The city's location gave it the competitive advantage of a shorter crossing to America than from other British or European ports. Technological innovations, such as the development of the steam engine, made the rapid growth of the manufacturing industry possible. Attracted to Glasgow by increased employment opportunities, migrant workers, particularly from rural Scotland and Ireland, swelled its population by the thousands. From around 13,000 in 1714 Glasgow's population expanded to over 200,000 by the 1830s, making it Britain's fourth most densely populated city.

There was great social change. Wealthy members of the expanding middle class were able to afford lavish lifestyles, but there were vast extremes of wealth and poverty. Mass production also brought manufactured products within reach of the working classes, heralding the start of the era of mass consumption.

Unrest led to repeated demands for social reform, because the political rights of the majority were extremely limited. The anti-slavery movement gained momentum in the late 1700s, which led to an Act of Parliament in 1807, abolishing the slave trade in the British Empire.

Leading Georgians have left a legacy in the architecture and cityscape. Andrew Buchanan, the Duke of Argyle, John Glassford and Archibald Ingram are just some of the prominent figures who still have streets named after them, and Virginia and Jamaica Streets directly recall the city's links with tobacco production in Britain's former colonies.

This book is divided into three sections. The first focuses on the merchants, the second on industries in Glasgow and the third on everyday life, particularly for the working classes.

Dr Anthony Lewis

Merchant system

The City of Glasgow benefited from international trading networks and trade with the Americas, Europe and India. Glasgow's leading businessmen were able to accumulate great wealth at home and abroad, which they invested in the city. This was the period when Glasgow's famous grid of streets and squares was laid out and built up with large houses, tenements and shops.

This 'New Town' and its public buildings, housing and industries were proclaimed with the cry 'Let Glasgow Flourish!' It echoed throughout the century in maps, books, buildings, civic awards and personal regalia, as Glasgow become a city of global significance, in terms of its business and industry.

Such success can be largely attributed to the 'Glasgow System', which depended on five key factors. The first of these was the merchants' focus on trading in profitable products like tobacco, sugar, textiles and ceramics. Second was their efficient logistical network, including shipping and canals, which allowed goods to be moved quickly. Third was the exploitation of slave labour in the Americas and the poor working classes in Britain to create a cheap labour economy. Then by creating their own banks and offering credit to each other they supported their associates. Lastly, by cultivating a business community of like-minded individuals they ensured that their wealth and commercial interests were protected.

By 1783 Glasgow's old Merchant Company was joined by Britain's very first Chamber of Commerce. A Town Council once dominated by aristocrats was now controlled by businessmen, who oversaw Glasgow's growth and contributed to its rise in influence and importance.

Detail from a guinea bank note, 1778
1894.147

'...Glasgow's famous grid of streets and squares was laid out ...'

The Glassford Family Portrait

John Glassford must have been deeply satisfied with life when this portrait was painted. He had extensive business holdings, but is perhaps best known for his American tobacco plantations. The Marlboro brand is named after the Virginia store that his company ran.

Glasgow was well placed geographically to benefit from a shorter sailing time to the Americas – ships could sail from Glasgow to the American colonies more quickly than they could from London or Liverpool, shaving several days off the voyage. Glassford was able to exploit this to his advantage. He controlled the international trade of millions of barrels of tobacco, thanks to his sailing fleet, which plied the Atlantic.

Glassford also exerted considerable influence with the city's Town Council through his brother-in-law, Lord Provost Archibald Ingram. He was involved in the creation of the Navigation Act, which led to the construction of the Forth and Clyde Canal in the 1760s. Glassford helped to negotiate loans for the building of the waterway, and the canal helped increase his profits by moving cargoes faster.

The Glassford Family Portrait,
about 1767–69
Archibald McLauchlan
2887

Glassford's vast wealth is hinted at through his possessions in this painting – the black slave boy standing behind his master's chair (see below), the horse-drawn carriage reflected in the mirror, the furniture, carpets, musical instruments and fine clothes. These were fashionable trappings of the highest quality and status in Glasgow society at the time. Although a deeply personal portrait, it is an example of how successful Glasgow's businessmen were in displaying their fortunes, ensuring that their wealth was seen by others.

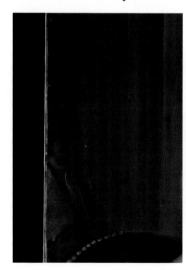

A detail of the black boy slave standing behind Glassford. His face had been obscured by discoloured varnish and dirt that had built up over the centuries.

9

Box, 1759
E.1971.1

Silver boxes inscribed with the city's coat of arms were used to keep prestigious documents in, such as burgess tickets, freedoms of the city or memberships of the Merchant Company and Chamber of Commerce. This one features the cry for which Glasgow is famous – 'Let Glasgow Flourish'.

Glasgow's Coat of Arms

The city's coat of arms consists of various symbols relating to its patron saint, St Mungo.

The bird was a pet which St Mungo restored to life. The tree symbolizes a camp fire which he relit using branches from nearby trees. The fish and the ring represent the story of St Mungo saving the honour of Queen Lanuoreth of Strathclyde. Her husband King Riderch demanded to see the ring he had given her, suspecting her of infidelity. St Mungo asked for a fish to be caught from the River Clyde – he knew that the missing ring would be found inside it, thus saving the Queen's honour and life. The bell is a gift the Pope gave to St Mungo after his many pilgrimages to Rome and in recognition of his good works.

Trade token, 1791
A.1940.28.B

In 1791 Gilbert Shearer was a cloth merchant living in Glasgow's Gallowgate. He issued this copper halfpenny trade token to his workforce as a form of payment. This allowed him to maximize his profits, as tokens such as this were only accepted in shops that Shearer controlled. The token shows the River God Clyde and the phrase '*nunquam arescere*' (never to run dry). Glasgow's coat of arms is on the other side.

Sphinxes,
1700–50
OG.1950.115.1-2

These two sphinxes would have stood upon a gateway
to a great Glasgow mansionhouse. They are thought to be
from the Shawfield Mansion, where millionaire merchant
John Glassford (1717–83) once lived. Statues such as these
symbolized that people were entering an elite space.

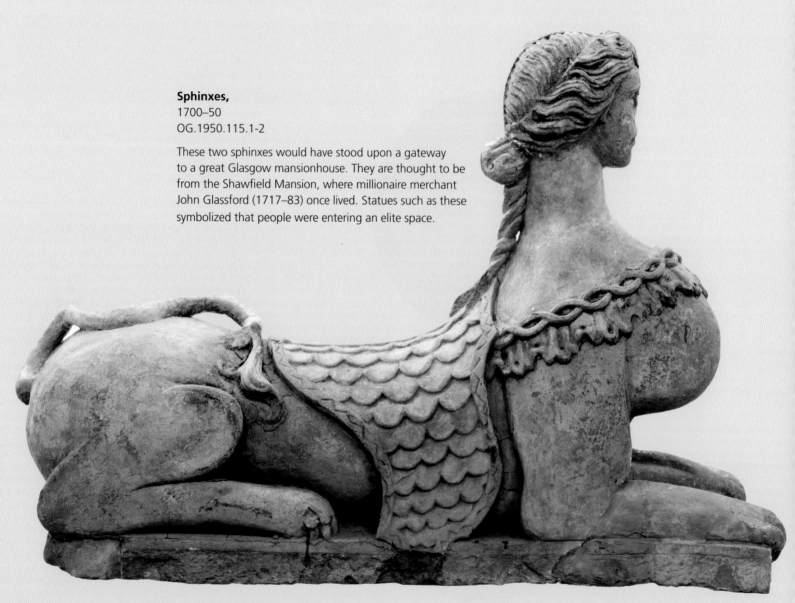

Conserving the Sphinxes

The sphinxes were carved from blonde sandstone in the 1700s. Over time they fractured into several separate components: torso, head and front legs. The surfaces had become obscured by plant growths, soil and black weathering accretions, as a result of being displayed outdoors and then stored over the past 200 years.

In order to make them fit for display the surfaces were cleaned with high-pressure steam and brushes, revealing residue of decorative paint and fittings for ornamentation to be attached. The separated fragments were fitted together with stainless steel rods to ensure structural stability, and areas of loss were filled and remodelled with Plaster of Paris. Missing pieces like the paws were cast in plaster from moulds taken from surviving components, and the tails were remodelled in clay and completed in Plaster of Paris. The white plaster fills were carved and colour-matched with modern acrylic paint to blend the new repairs into the overall appearance.

13

Mask

This plaster mask comes from a house that architect and businessman Allan Dreghorn (1706–64) constructed on Clyde Street, during the late 1750s to early 1760s. The mask once sat above a doorway to a drawing or dining room, and was part of a greater scheme of plasterwork which Dreghorn's long-term business partner, the plasterer Thomas Clayton, designed and installed.

Dreghorn and Clayton made their fortunes through the rebuilding of Glasgow and the erection of mansions and palaces in the surrounding area. Clayton was employed by William Adam during the building and decoration of the 5th Duke of Hamilton's now demolished Hamilton Palace and his hunting lodge at nearby Chatelherault. He was also responsible for the plasterwork in the Duke of Atholl's Blair Castle in Perthshire.

The pair joined stonemason Mungo Naismith and sculptor David Cation to form the team that designed and built Glasgow's Town Hall. They worked on the church St Andrew's in the Square, the Town Hospital and the Assembly Rooms. Dreghorn's name appears in notebooks connected to the construction of Pollok House in 1752. Today it is Glasgow's finest surviving mansion.

Dreghorn's own house – lavishly decorated and outfitted to the highest standards of the day – proclaimed his success not just as a prominent architect or tradesman, but also as a banker. This was unusual and put Dreghorn in a different social circle to his tradesmen peers. Not only could he plan a new Glasgow but he had the means to finance the work as well.

Guests visiting the mansion who were familiar with the homes of dukes and aristocrats may have recognized Clayton's work. Such plaster masks appeared in Dreghorn's home and in his Town Hall piazza – surviving examples are known better today as the Tontine Heads (opposite).

Keen-eyed and knowledgeable visitors may even have realized that this mask was the same as one used in Blair Castle's drawing room, making Dreghorn's mansion appear on a par with Scotland's first rank of fashionable aristocratic homes.

Mask, 1750–60s
Made by Thomas Clayton
TEMP.9359.1

Archibald, 3rd Duke of Argyll

Archibald Campbell, 3rd Duke of Argyll (1682–1761) was once known as the most powerful man in Scotland. Here he sits in his robes as the Keeper of the Great Seal of Scotland, which allowed him to authorize decisions on behalf of the King.

In 1727 he helped found the Royal Bank of Scotland and acted as its first governor. Glasgow Town Council purchased this portrait in 1749 from the famed artist Allan Ramsay for its new Town Hall. It hung alongside portraits of monarchs, indicating the city's respect for both the Duke's political power and the Hanoverian monarchy.

The dedication of Argyle Street, one of the city's main throughfares, further suggests the reverence with which Argyll was viewed, as a member of the Privy Council and Keeper of the Great Seal.

Archibald, 3rd Duke of Argyll,
1749
Allan Ramsay
471

Punch bowl, 1716

E.1946.87.im

Rum punches were commonly served at parties and formal assemblies. This punch bowl was made in London in 1716. Wealthy Scots would have recognized it as a typically attractive, fashionable and exclusive piece of silverware often used by the city's elite.

Guinea bank note, 1778

1894.147

Glasgow's Ship, Thistle and Arms banks were founded between 1749 and 1761. This note from the Arms Bank bore the city's coat of arms, and like the others, promoted Glasgow's name and financial interests. Allan Dreghorn was a founding partner of the Ship Bank and John Glassford was a founding member of both the Thistle and Arms banks.

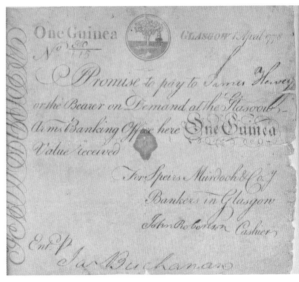

Organ, 1762
1918.58

Music organs were novelties in Glasgow's churches in the 1700s and they were also built for Freemasonic lodges. James Watt was asked to build a music organ in 1762 but his patron remains unknown. This organ is attributed to Watt and was later owned by the famous Glasgow merchant Archibald McLellan.

The organ was conserved in 2014 thanks to a grant from The Leche Trust and many genereous public donations.

Chippendale table,
about 1750
E.1979.66

As Glasgow expanded and great houses were built the demand for furniture increased. Local builders and furniture makers met this demand, producing work which followed London's fashions for those who could not afford to buy directly from the capital.

This was made possible through pattern books of designs and amongst the most popular was Thomas Chippendale's *The Gentlemen and Cabinet Maker's Director* (1754). This table is an example of a Chippendale table which only the elite could afford to have made. It was made for the Maxwells of Pollok House, which still stands in Pollok Park today. Many other Georgian objects can still be seen in Pollok House, above right.

Teapot

Teapot, about 1750
E.1937.75.c

African slaves were the principal workforce producing tobacco, sugar, indigo and rice for Glasgow's businessmen. Millions of people were sold as slaves, then shipped from Africa to America and the Caribbean and forced to work on plantations. Very few became domestic slaves and fewer still lived in Glasgow itself.

Only the very rich had personal slaves in their homes, and it indicates Glasgow's mercantile wealth and status that there is evidence of slavery in the city. John Glassford's family portrait shows a black slave looking on, and the city's archives and newspapers carried stories of some who were in service to other families or had taken their chances at running away.

Black slaves were commonly trained in a trade, such as barbering or carpentry but they were also seen as a status symbol of success and wealth.

This earthenware teapot was made by Wedgwood's factories in the mid eighteenth century. It was not hand painted but had a transfer print applied to it. This shows that it was intended to be inexpensive to produce and buy.

The message behind the teapot could be read in diffferent ways. It might represent an endorsement of the slave trade – not only through its depiction of a black boy, in livery, attending a couple – but in the ceramic itself, in the sense that it was readily available and affordable. On the other hand it may have encouraged wider debate about slavery and its potential abolition.

A View of Glasgow from the South East,
date unknown
Made by the Foulis Academy
PP.1981.33.22

The familiar skyline from the south east included towers of public buildings, houses, the River Clyde and its bridge. People are working by the river and platoons of soldiers can be seen performing their drill in the distance.

The Foulis Academy was a successful publishing company that produced prints of Glasgow from various compass points. They were inexpensive and were available from the city's bookshops and retailers.

Susan Euphemia, wife of the 10th Duke of Hamilton and Brandon, date unknown
PR.1978.6

Susan Euphemia Beckford was a wealthy woman in her own right before her marriage to the 10th Duke of Hamilton in 1810. She was a patron of the arts, an accomplished pianist, and later a patron to composer Frédéric Chopin, who played at Hamilton Palace in 1848.

A proposed design for Glasgow's Court House
D-TC13/4001

This drawing shows the front elevation of an unsuccessful submission by architect Robert Reid to design Glasgow's Justiciary Court in 1809. Glasgow was the centre of the West of Scotland's legal and justice system. The scale of the proposed new court houses reflected this status. Architects from Edinburgh and Glasgow competed for the contract to design and build the court house in the early 1800s. Edinburgh's Robert Reid offered these particular designs, but he eventually lost out to the architect William Stark.

The Royal Bank of Scotland Building about 1817, formerly William Cunninghame of Lainshaw's Glasgow Mansion, from *Glasgow Delineated*, 1839 edition

GC 914/1435GLA

By the mid 1770s William Cunninghame had become an immensely wealthy tobacco merchant. He proclaimed his success by building himself a big house at the terminus of Ingram Street. The house dominated the vista as though it were a church to commerce. Here it is shown after it was converted into a bank. It is now Glasgow's Gallery of Modern Art.

Snuff box

Glasgow was famous for its tobacco trade and it would not have been uncommon to see a Glaswegian merchant offer a friend or acquaintance snuff, a refined powder form of tobacco, to ingest. Snuff was kept in fine boxes which allowed their owners to declare their wealth and interests through the materials used to make them and the emblems they were decorated with.

This is a tortoiseshell snuff box with silver collars, scrolls and a delicate gold strand around the outer edge. It dates to the 1720s and carries an embossed and engraved bust of King George I on it to announce its owner's loyalties to the Hanoverian monarch.

It was common for politicians or merchants to go to Hanover and manage their affairs in Glasgow by post. In July 1725 George Bogle of Daldowie was allowed to kiss the King's hand in Hanover, securing his assent to trade in tobacco and sugar.

During this time news spread of severe riots in Glasgow which had destroyed Glasgow MP Daniel Campbell's town mansion. A fire incinerated up to 40 more houses and was suspected of being a Scottish Jacobite plot. Demonstrations of loyalty and service – such as carrying a snuffbox decorated with the King's profile – were considered necessary in return for patronage.

Snuff box, about 1720
1883.32.aw

'...snuff, a refined powder form of tobacco...'

Old Glasgow Bridge,
about 1817
John Knox
OG.1955.119

This painting shows the Broomielaw to Glasgow Green. Stretched along Clyde Street are the Cathedral, the Town's Hospital, the Merchants' House with its prominent steeple, Allan Dreghorn's mansion and the judiciary Courthouse and Jail, amongst other key buildings. The signs of imminent industrialization are on the horizon to the left, with the smoking cone of the glassworks at the Broomielaw and the factory chimneys of Anderston.

Isobel McDonald

Industry

In the early 1700s Glasgow was a small market town surrounded by agricultural lands interspersed with villages. However unprecedented industrial and agricultural developments during the Georgian period transformed the region. Such change was often funded by wealthy merchants with the profits from their overseas trade. But it was also driven by exciting new ideas, innovations and the growing availability of a large workforce.

Textile production was the key local industry during the time. The increasing demand for linen and later cotton cloth led to the establishment of weaving villages such as Anderston and Calton, where large numbers of self-employed weavers clustered together. But Scottish engineer James Watt's improvements to the steam engine allowed textile manufacture to be mechanized, which rapidly led to the construction of large cotton mills in Glasgow. Steam power was increasingly being used in other industries as well, boosting the development of local ironworking and engineering companies.

A wide range of industries flourished in Glasgow during this period. Those mentioned in the Statistical Account published in the 1790s include pottery, hat-making, glass, soap and candle making, sugar refining, rope and cord-making, snuff mills, iron founding and engineering and various extractive industries, including coal, lime, alum, stone quarries, and later iron ore.

River Clyde from Clydebrae, 1843
Michael Honeyman
685.a

Woodside near Glasgow

Woodside Mill was built on the banks of the
River Kelvin in the 1780s by William Gillespie,
who employed around 400 men, women and
children there. Gillespie hired Henry Houldsworth,
a Nottingham man, to manage the mill and
Houldsworth later bought it.

Woodside was the only water-powered cotton
spinning mill in Glasgow, and suffered from water
shortages in the summer months, which limited its
output. The development of steam power transformed
the textile industry in Glasgow over a very short period,
freeing it from the limitations of water power. The first
steam-powered mill was built for William Scott and
Co. at Springfield in 1792 and by 1831 there were 107
steam-powered mills in Glasgow.

Factory shifts were long, and the work was
generally poorly paid, tedious and unhealthy,
organized to suit the machines, not the workforce.
Mill employees were usually women, children
and immigrants. Workers typically suffered from
respiratory problems, brought on by the extreme
heat and dusty conditions.

Woodside near Glasgow,
date unknown
Andrew Donaldson
OG.1951.417.0.1

34

Salmon fishing at Govan,
about 1820, artist unknown
Temp.5899

Salmon fishing at Govan was a
significant concern. Boundary
stones were laid out to show
the limits of the various
fisheries and salmon netting
continued until the mid 1800s.

Putters or Trolley-boys in England, 1869
© Science Museum /
Science & Society Picture
Library

Working in mines was just
one of many dangerous
jobs done by British children
during the 1800s.

Miner's token, pre-1832
PP.1982.46.5

This token is from Westmuir
Colliery, Shettleston. It was owned
by the Gray family, who became
major local coal producers. They
modernized Westmuir by installing
a wind pump for drainage in 1737,
and later a steam engine in 1768.
It is not clear what this token may
have been used for but it may
possibly be connected with tallying
each miner's daily haul of coal.

Dress

Dress,
about 1800
E.2013.7

This dress is made from white figured muslin with a geometric design and dates from about 1800. It would have been produced on a lappet loom, a type of loom that uses additional warp threads to create such patterns. The cloth was hand woven by a local weaver for Brown and Sharp of Paisley, and shows the kind of fine materials being produced in the West of Scotland.

Cloth manufacturers made up pattern books containing samples of the different fabrics they sold. The sample for this dress is in one of Brown and Sharp's pattern books held by Paisley Museum and Art Galleries.

© Renfrewshire Arts and Museums

A View of Glasgow

Most of the land that lies within modern Glasgow's boundaries was agricultural during the Georgian period. This image of haystacks near Glasgow Cathedral shows how undeveloped even the central parts of Glasgow were in 1760.

In the late 1700s locally-grown crops included wheat, oats, peas, beans, flax, barley, potatoes and turnips. Dairy farming was also important – in Eastwood parish, for example, two thirds of the land was used as pasture, and only one third for crops. Glasgow's growing population provided a steady market for foodstuffs, and farmers used the city's night soil as manure. Fresh fruit and vegetables came from the market gardens and orchards which flourished on the outskirts of the city.

Robert Paul (1739–70) studied at The Foulis Academy of Art in Glasgow and produced an important series of engravings depicting the city in the mid 1700s

A *View taken from the West of the Cathedral of Glasgow,* date unknown
Robert Paul
A.1940.7.ab.11

41

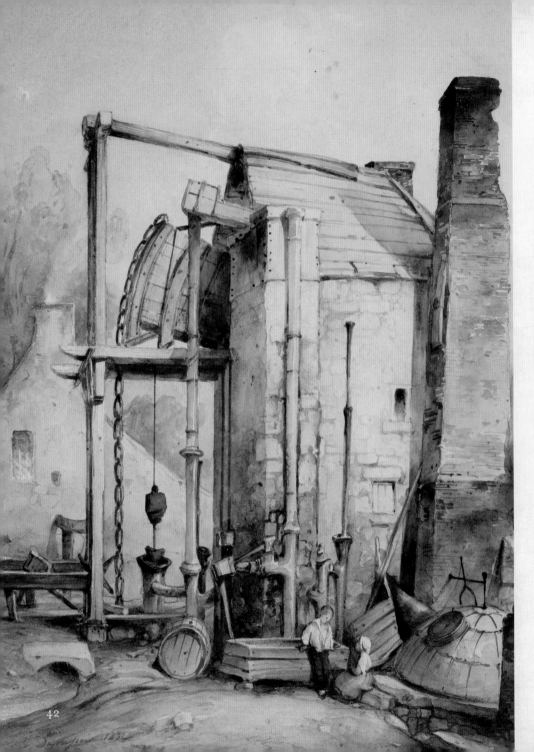

Machine à vapeur à Glasgow Ecosse,
1832
Francois Joseph Dupressoir
T.2007.14

This steam engine was part of a distillery near Glasgow. The image shows just how big early engines were – and yet for the children nearby they seem an everyday part of the landscape.

This token shows the Phoenix Foundry building. The Foundry was established around 1797 by Thomas Edington. It produced high-quality ornamental ironwork, including the gates at the Glasgow Necropolis, pictured on the last page of this book. Tokens were used to pay workers, forcing them to use shops connected to the foundry.

Token, 1817
PP.1982.46.5

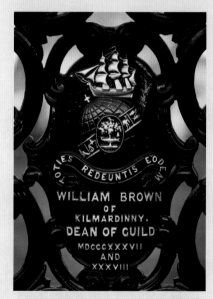

A detail from the gates to
Glasgow Necropolis.

Portrait of George MacIntosh

George MacIntosh was born in Roskeen, Ross-shire. Although his father's farm kept the family comfortably, as the fourth son George had to seek his fortune elsewhere. He moved to Glasgow to work as a junior clerk at a tannery. By 1773 MacIntosh was running his own business, employing 500 boot and shoemakers.

However MacIntosh was best known for developing the dye industry in Glasgow. In 1777 he established a cudbear manufactory at Dennistoun. Made from lichen, cudbear is used to dye wool and silk red. To protect trade secrets, only immigrant Gaelic speakers were hired as workers and the manufactory and the workers' housing were surrounded by a high wall.

In 1785 MacIntosh was a partner with David Dale in setting up a Turkey red dyeworks at Barrowfield. This red dye was used on cotton. MacIntosh's son Charles invented a process for waterproofing cloth, giving rise to the MacIntosh coat.

Portrait of George MacIntosh,
about 1800–07
1903

'... the workers were immigrant Gaelic speakers...'

45

Tennant's Chemical Works,
date unknown
PP.1975.63

During the 1700s cloth was bleached white by being boiled in stale urine and then left out in sunlight for several months in a bleachfield.

  Around 1788 Charles Tennant opened a bleachfield in Darnley but he realized that this bleaching process was slow and inefficient. In 1799 Tennant patented bleaching powder. He built a bleach factory at St Rollox, which by the 1830s was the biggest chemical works in the world.

This detail from p.53 shows women bleaching linen by the river – back-breaking work!

Dress, about 1824–26
E.1945.66.b

We think that this muslin dress was
tamboured (decorated) with green
wool in Anderston. Tambouring was
usually done by women and girls
working at home. In 1791, 105,000
people worked at tambouring across
Scotland.

Fiona Hayes

Daily Life

'Most people drank ale as water was not safe to drink...'

The Trongate of Glasgow in 1774, 1774
James Brown, after Maclure & Macdonald
1906.126.b

What was daily life like in this period for most Glaswegians, who were not part of the merchant elite?

Home could be a tenement, cottage or a room in a lodging house. For the homeless there was the poorhouse at the Town's Hospital. Most people drank ale as water was not safe to drink. Soup, oats and bread were staple foods, supplemented by cheese, fish, vegetables and meat, depending on income. These were bought from stalls set up near the town centre on market days. For a fee, dairy cows could be grazed on Glasgow Green.

In the late 1700s radical groups debated new ideas about democracy and equality which became a call for electoral reform. Add into the mix industrial protest about falling wages and rising prices and Glasgow was a volatile place.

Working people set up friendly societies to put aside money to draw upon during hard times. They started trade unions to protect their wages from being cut during recession.

Religion played an important role in people's lives. When people were not working there were sports like bowling and curling. During Glasgow Fair each July the shows came to Glasgow Green.

OBJECT IN FOCUS
Partick Drum

The sound of this drum regulated daily life and broadcast news in Partick, which in the 1700s was a village beside Glasgow. The drum was part of community life and functioned as a public timekeeper. At 5am it indicated the time to get up and at 9pm it heralded the end of the day.

The drummer was elected and paid by the villagers. The drum was used to signal public announcements and villagers could also pay the drummer to make announcements on their behalf. It is decorated with Masonic symbols and was used to lead processions for Partick St Mary's Masonic Lodge as well as Partick Ploughmen's Friendly Society's annual election parade.

The drum was made in London by Robert Horne, who was in business from around 1770 to 1806. Partick was not the only town or village to have a public drum but as the village grew it gradually became obsolete. By the mid nineteenth century the drum was no longer heard in the streets.

'... The drum signalled public announcements ...'

Partick Drum,
date unknown
Made by Robert Horne
Temp.8067

Sampler,
early 19th century
Made by Catherine Gaunt
OG.1949.30.h

Girls made samplers to demonstrate their sewing skills, an important part of female education. The Institution for Orphans and Destitute Girls was established in the 1820s. It gave the girls a home and an education, and trained them for domestic service.

Penny a Week School –
***Goat Burn**, about 1800*
PP.1978.101.8

This school was built in 1790 with subscriptions from 80 local inhabitants. Pupils paid a penny a week to attend, learning reading, writing and arithmetic, with '… sewing if deemed advisable; the Bible and the Shorter Catechism to be used daily'.

FLAG

This flag would have been an amazing sight at the Reform demonstrations in the 1830s. It is a large flag, measuring 1.65 metres high by 2.15 metres wide – in other words, it was made to make a statement!

The flag is full of recognizable symbols from the time. This image shows the back of the flag and represents the people marching behind it. We know that it was carried by weavers because it features their symbol, a large cat with a shuttle in its mouth.

On the front of the flag is Britannia, a symbol of Britain. In one hand she holds a staff with a liberty cap, a reference to the French Revolution ideas of liberty and equality. It suggests that these marchers were on the radical wing of the Reform movement. The ship *Reform* is shown in the foreground on the facing page.

An estimated 100,000 to 150,000 people took part in the demonstration on Glasgow Green on April 1832 to urge Parliament to pass the Reform Bill. Even allowing for some exaggeration, this is a huge turnout.

The flag carries the slogan, 'Scotland's Sons Shall Aye Be Free' along the top, echoing a popular tavern song and reflects concerns about liberty. 'Free Trade to all the World' is written along the bottom, in protest at restrictive trade practises, blamed for high food prices and profiteering.

'... it was made to make a statement! ...'

Flag, about 1830
A.1943.70

55

Old Glasgow Cross

John Knox's 1826 painting of Old Glasgow Cross, also known as *The Trongate*, shows what a busy, bustling place Glasgow had become. Knox (1778–1845) was a Glasgow painter and art teacher.

At this time the street is a place for people to meet and chat and there is a cross section of Glasgow society to be seen here, from well-dressed women to barefoot children. Street sellers, porters and carters go about their work. Mail and passenger coaches link the town centre with places like London, Edinburgh and Ayr. The ground floor shops with goods in their windows were a new retail development and showed Glasgow was a modern town. The shop names shown in the painting can be found in the Glasgow Post Office Directory of this time.

The Tolbooth, the building on the right with the steeple, had been the town jail. Beside it is the arcaded Tontine where the town's merchants would meet for business. The steeple of the Tron Church is seen on the left.

'... there is a cross section of society to be seen here ...'

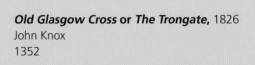

Old Glasgow Cross or The Trongate, 1826
John Knox
1352

57

Deacon's box

The Glasgow Journeymen Bakers' Friendly Society kept their documents and funds secure inside this mahogany box. When the Society was created in 1765 they had this box made at a cost of £2.12.6d.

In a period when there was no official welfare provision, friendly societies run by and for their members provided financial support to working people when they were unable to work. Members regularly paid in subscriptions against the time when they might need help. Records kept in this box show that the Society also paid widows' pensions and funeral charges. Each of the three officer bearers had a key and all three had to be present to open the box.

The painted front shows bakers in their working clothes with the tools of their craft. The figure on the left holds a wooden oven paddle for baking bread and the figure on the right holds a flail for threshing wheat.

The Society used this box until it disbanded in 1911 after national insurance was introduced.

'they had this box made at a cost of £2.12.6d'

Deacon's box, 1765
1911.99.a

Not all businesses were run by men, as this portrait shows. The Glasgow Post Office directories and letters of the period show that women were running businesses. The 1801 directory lists 26 women grocers (listed opposite) but none were recorded in a 1787 version. The women were either married or widows. It was not until 1998 that Glasgow's Chamber of Commerce had its first female president, Marilyn Orcharton.

This shop keeper's gold and jet jewellery, fine muslin dress and tidy well-stocked shop all hint at her wealth and status. She looks out confidently as she places coins or tokens on the counter.

She is selling lemons, tea and sugar cones wrapped in black paper. The cabinets behind her probably contained valuable spices such as pepper, nutmeg, mace and cloves. Lemons and sugar are the main ingredients of Glasgow Punch, along with rum.

The secret of a good Glasgow punch, known at the time as 'mingling juice', is making a sherbet first. This is a fine mix of sugar, lemon juice and water. Then add one part rum to five or six of the sherbet and enjoy!

Brown, Mrs. William, grocer, 91, High-street
Bruce, Mrs. J., grocer, 285, High-street
Campbell, Mrs., grocer, 229, High-street
Chalmers, Mrs John, grocer, 23, Canon-street
Clarke, Mrs. D., grocer, 31, Wilson-street
Cochrane, Mrs., grocer, 15, Canon-street
Craig, Mrs., grocer, 300, Gallowgate
Cumming, Mrs., grocer, 2, Jamaica-street
Forman, Mrs Ralph, vintner & grocer, Spoutmouth
Hutton, Mrs., grocer, 77, Bridgegate
Jaffrey, Mrs., grocer, 102, George-street
Jones, Mrs., grocer, 118, Saltmarket
Limont, Mrs. J. grocer, 62, Argyll-street
Mack, Mrs., grocer, 75, Saltmarket
McFarlane, Mrs. Robert, grocer, 28, Candelriggs
McNeil, Mrs D., grocer, 46 Argyll-street
McComb, Mrs., grocer, 119, Argyll-street
McKenzie, Mrs., grocer, 14, New Wynd
Miller, Mrs., grocer, 354, Gallowgate
Milligan, Mrs. George, grocer, 42, New Wynd
Monteith, Mrs., grocer, 12, Stockwell
Mosman, Mrs., grocer, 126, High-street
Shearer, Mrs., grocer, 64 Stockwell
Sym, Mrs., grocer, 95 High-street
Turcan, Mrs., grocer, 9, Stockwell
Walker, Mrs., grocer, 64, Saltmarket

The Woman Shop Keeper,
1790–1800
Unknown artist
Temp.7685

A View of Glasgow looking down the Clyde,
1808
J Brooks
PP.1981.145

There is a lively cross section of daily life in this watercolour of Glasgow Green. Fashionable and wealthy people 'promenade' or walk out to be seen. Meanwhile the linen bleachers and milkmaids are hard at work on the Green.

Professor of Swimming's medal, 1837
1876.167.[1]

This medal shows swimmers at a spot called the Dominie's Hole on the River Clyde, by Glasgow Green. The Town Council had installed facilities there for swimming, including springboards, benches for clothes and stone paving to stop swimmers' feet from getting muddy.

Left: The Dominie's Hole today.

Detail from *The Trongate of Glasgow in 1774*
1774, James Brown, after Maclure & Macdonald
OG.1951.417.as

Water had to be fetched and carried from a well or street pump. In the early 1700s the Town Council began to convert the town wells to pumps to make it easier to get the water. In August 1730 it agreed that 'a pump be put upon the Tronegate well'.

Handbill, During the Fair
TD/462

Glasgow Fair is an ancient local holiday that takes place in July. It dates from the 1100s. Originally a cattle fair, it later became known for its shows and entertainments. 'The Phenomenon of Nature', international showman Monsieur Chabert, brought his death-defying act to Glasgow Fair. The Fair crowds could see him walk into a hot oven with raw meat, stay inside long enough for it to cook and then come out unharmed. He also swallowed poisons like phosphorous.

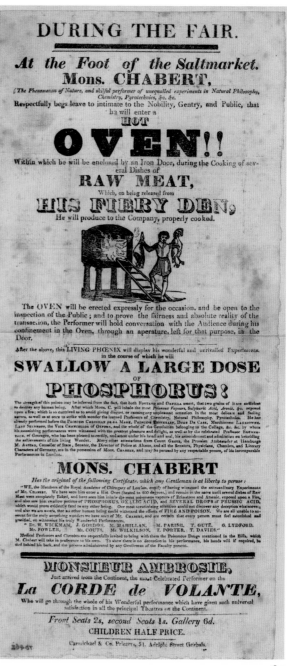

Glasgow Fair, Northern Looking Glass
© The University of Glasgow Library, Special Collections

By the early 1800s Glasgow Fair was evolving from a market fair to a spectacular feast of entertainment with theatre shows, circus and rides. This 1825 *Northern Looking Glass* illustration captures the excitement of the fair as the show-men advertise their shows to the crowds gathered in the Saltmarket.

Communion token, 1725
A.1945.39.[3]

Presbyterian churches, such as Glasgow Cathedral (below), issued communion tokens to their members to show that they were part of the church and could take part in Holy Communion, the most sacred part of the church service. This 1725 token features an early version of Glasgow's coat of arms.

Ring, 1794
PP.1987.36.1

Standing up for their beliefs came at a cost for those involved in radical politics. William Skirving, General Secretary of the Friends of the People, was charged with encouraging rebellion and transported to Australia in 1794. His wife Rachel gave him this ring with a lock of hair. She never saw him again, as he died in March 1796.

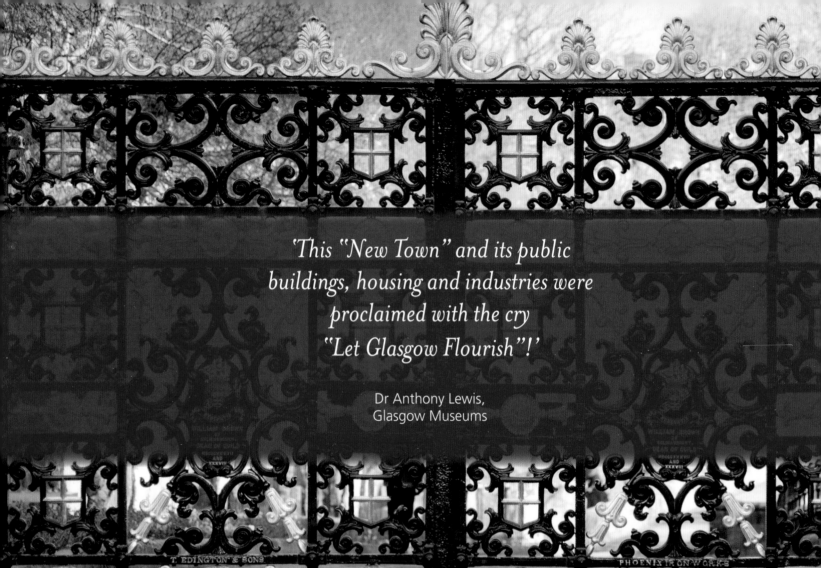

'This "New Town" and its public
buildings, housing and industries were
proclaimed with the cry
"Let Glasgow Flourish"!'

Dr Anthony Lewis,
Glasgow Museums